CONTENTS

Welcome to the Northern Mariana Islands

Håfa adai (huh-fah-day). That's how to say hello in Chamorro, one of the main languages spoken on the Northern Mariana Islands. The Northern Mariana Islands are located in the western Pacific Ocean. On a world map, they appear as 14 dots between Hawaii and the Philippines. Their official name is the **Commonwealth** of the Northern Mariana Islands, or CNMI. The CNMI is a U.S. territory.

More than 50,000 people call the CNMI home. Most residents live on the island of Saipan. Some live on the islands of Tinian and Rota. The other islands are sparsely populated.

The people of the CNMI come from many different places. More than half of the residents were born somewhere else. The islands' history and geography explain how this happened.

Territories of the United States

NORTHERN MARIANA ISLANDS

Elissa Bongiorno

PowerKiDS press

Published in 2025 by The Rosen Publishing Group, Inc.
2544 Clinton Street, Buffalo, NY 14224

First Edition

Editor: Therese Shea
Book Design: Rachel Rising

Photo Credits: Cover ArtNat/Shutterstock.com; Cover, pp. 1, 3–32 boromvit tatasai/Shutterstock.com; Cover, pp. 1, 3–32 P-fotography/Shutterstock.com; Cover, pp. 1, 7, 9, 15, 17, 19, 25, 29 https://commons.wikimedia.org/wiki/File:Flag_of_the_Northern_Mariana_Islands.svg; p. 4 railway fx/Shutterstock.com;p. 5 Rainer Lesniewski/Shutterstock.com; pp. 5 (bottom), 17, 28 RaksyBH/Shutterstock.com; p. 5 Waterbear/Shutterstock.com; p. 6 https://en.m.wikipedia.org/wiki/File:Ash_Plume_and_Ash_Fall_of_May_1994_Eruption_of_Mount_Pagan_volcano_in_Northern_Mariana_Islands.jpg; p. 7 Designua/Shutterstock.com; p. 9 https://en.wikipedia.org/wiki/File:AgrihanNASA.jpg; p. 11 (bottom) https://en.m.wikipedia.org/wiki/File:A_Seabee_removes_debris_from_a_road_during_recovery._(44751228255).jpg; p. 11 (top) Elena11/Shutterstock.com; p. 12 Oakland Images/Shutterstock.com; p. 13 Mark J Meyers/Shutterstock.com; p. 14 Tamil Selvam/Shutterstock.com; p. 15 Mano's/Shutterstock.com; p. 19 https://en.wikipedia.org/wiki/File:Stamp_Mariana_Islands_1901_20pf.jpg; p. 21 https://en.m.wikipedia.org/wiki/File:LVTs_move_toward_Saipan,_past_bombarding_cruisers,_on_15_June_1944_(80-G-231838).jpg; p. 23 https://commons.wikimedia.org/wiki/File:Atomic_bomb_1945_mission_heb.jpg; p. 25 zmotions/Shutterstock.com; p. 26 zefart/Shutterstock.com; p. 27 Triphibian Productions/Shutterstock.com.

Library of Congress Cataloging-in-Publication Data

Names: Bongiorno, Elissa, author.
Title: Northern Mariana Islands / Elissa Bongiorno.
Description: Buffalo, New York : PowerKids Press, [2025] | Series: Territories of the United States | Includes bibliographical references and index.
Identifiers: LCCN 2024000262 (print) | LCCN 2024000263 (ebook) | ISBN 9781725329119 (library binding) | ISBN 9781725329096 (paperback) | ISBN 9781725329126 (ebook)
Subjects: LCSH: Northern Mariana Islands--Juvenile literature.
Classification: LCC DU643 .B66 2025 (print) | LCC DU643 (ebook) | DDC 996.7--dc23/eng/20240131
LC record available at https://lccn.loc.gov/2024000262
LC ebook record available at https://lccn.loc.gov/2024000263

Manufactured in the United States of America

Some of the images in this book illustrate individuals who are models. The depictions do not imply actual situations or events.

CPSIA Compliance Information: Batch #CSPK25. For further information contact Rosen Publishing at 1-800-237-9932.

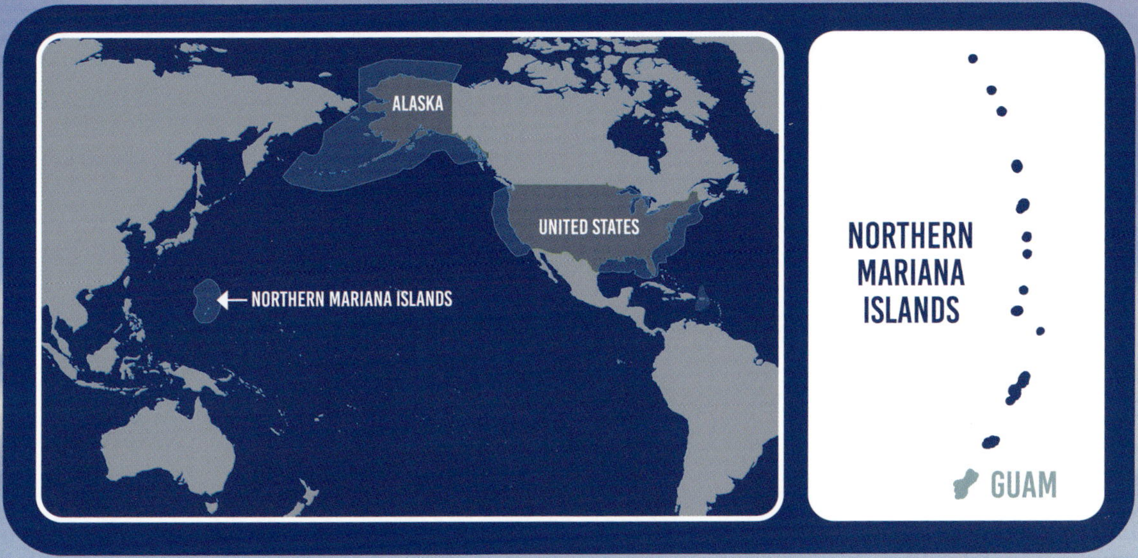

Together, the islands of the CNMI are about 179 square miles (463 sq km), or about 2.5 times the size of Washington, D.C.

Born from Volcanoes

The islands of the CNMI and Guam, a separate U.S. territory, together form an **archipelago** called the Mariana Islands or simply the Marianas. The CNMI and Guam are separated politically, meaning they operate under different governments. However, scientists group them as an archipelago because of their location and geologic origins.

The older, southern islands, where most people live, were made by molten rock following volcanic eruptions more than 16 million years ago. They're now covered in limestone from ancient coral reefs. The northern islands are newer, formed by volcanic eruptions in the past 4,000 years.

Where do these volcanoes come from? Earth's outer layer is made up of giant pieces of rock called tectonic plates. Where the Marianas are located, the Pacific Plate is slowly moving under the Philippine Plate.

MOUNT PAGAN VOLCANO

THE DEEPEST SPOT IN THE WORLD

Far beneath the Pacific Ocean's surface lies the Mariana Trench. At the southern end is an area called Challenger Deep. It's the deepest part of the ocean at around 36,070 feet (10,994 m). If Mount Everest, the tallest mountain above sea level, could fit inside Challenger Deep, there would still be about 7,000 feet (2,134 m) between the peak and the water's surface! Only a few people have visited the Mariana Trench. They undertake the dangerous journey in underwater vehicles called submersibles.

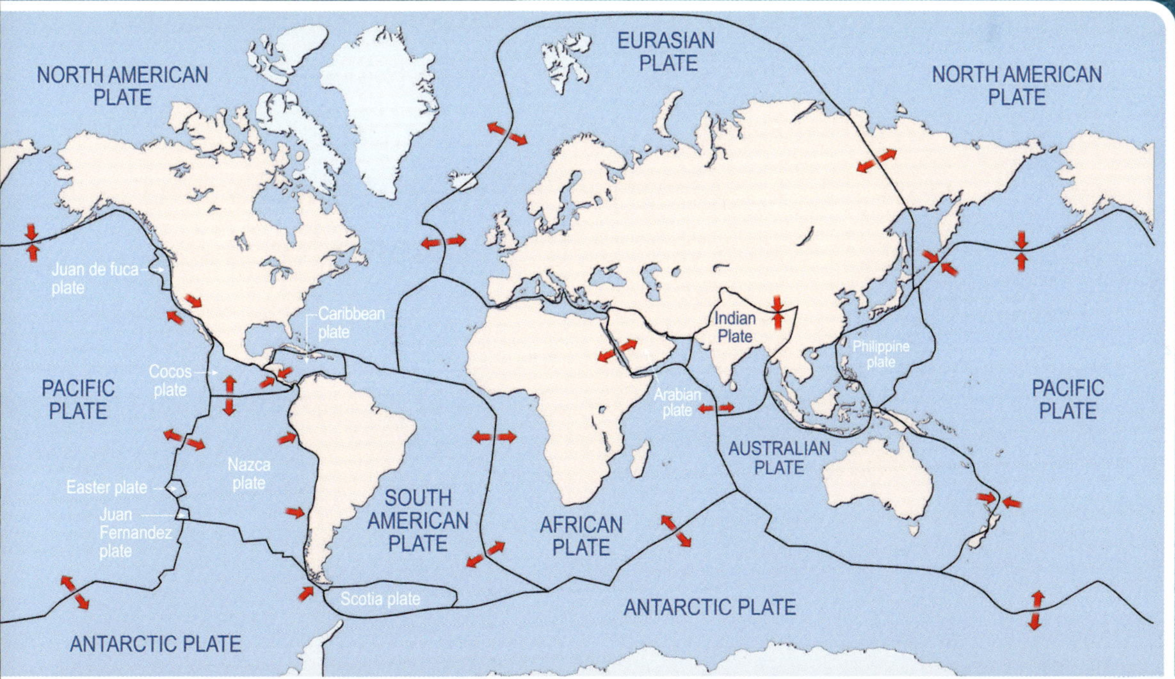

The movements of tectonic plates can explain some geologic events, such as volcanic eruptions and earthquakes.

The Pacific Plate creates volcanoes as well as earthquakes all around its edges. These form a sort of curved area often called the Ring of Fire. The Northern Mariana Islands are in the Ring of Fire.

Nineteen active volcanoes are located in the CNMI. According to scientists, two of those have a high chance of erupting. One of these volcanoes is on Pagan Island. This island is actually two connected stratovolcanoes, which are volcanoes made up of layers of ash and cooled lava. Mount Pagan in the north of the island is the most active. Its last large eruption was in 1981, causing the sparse population to leave. Smaller eruptions have occurred since then, including in 2021. Scientists using **satellites** and other research tools watch the volcano for signs of activity.

Territorial Truths ☆☆☆☆☆

Because the Northern Mariana Islands are located in an area with earthquakes and volcanoes, tsunamis are a danger. People are advised to move inland when they feel a quake or hear a warning signal.

ANATAHAN ERUPTS

Another CNMI volcano with a moderate risk of eruption is on Anatahan, which is in the middle of the Northern Marianas. The volcano began showing signs of activity in 1990, forcing the 23 people who lived on the island to leave. In 2003, the volcano had its first recorded eruption. Ash and steam spewed into the air, while lava flowed down the mountainsides. The volcano also erupted in 2004 and 2005. These eruptions have changed the features of the island.

The forested island of Agrigan (Agrihan) is a stratovolcano, whose top is the highest point in the CNMI. Agrigan is a high-threat volcano with a giant caldera, or crater, visible here.

Wild Weather

The climate of the CNMI is tropical, which means it's warm and rainy. This is because the Northern Mariana Islands are near the equator, where the sun shines most directly. It's also because the islands are surrounded by the ocean. There is a dry season, from December to June, and a wet season, when it rains more, from July to November. The average temperature is 84°F (29°C).

The CNMI also has a typhoon season, which runs from about July to January. Typhoons, called hurricanes in other parts of the world, are powerful, circular storms that develop over warm oceans. They can build in just a few days and produce winds stronger than 120 miles (193 km) per hour. Typhoons can cause extreme wind damage and flooding.

Territorial Truths ☆☆☆☆☆

On the islands of Tinian and Saipan, two people were killed and more than 130 were injured during Typhoon Yutu in 2018.

In 2018, a typhoon called Yutu was the strongest recorded storm to hit the Mariana Islands. Winds gusted as fast as 180 miles (290 km) per hour.

Animals, Land and Sea

The Northern Mariana Islands are home to a wide variety of animal life. Some species are endemic to the CNMI, meaning they live only on these islands and nowhere else in the world. Some of these species are **endangered** birds, including the Mariana crow. The destruction of this bird's habitat by typhoons and human activity is one reason for its disappearance. Another is the accidental introduction of the brown tree snake to the islands. The U.S. government is trying to stop this **invasive species** by using poisoned bait and snake-detecting dogs.

Some areas of the CNMI are set aside to allow birds and other native species to live away from people and their activities. This includes I'Chenchon Park Bird Sanctuary on the eastern side of the island of Rota.

MARIANA CROW

Territorial Truths

The brown tree snake is believed to be responsible for the local extinction of 10 bird species on the nearby island of Guam.

The Mariana fruit dove is the Northern Mariana Islands' official bird. Also known as the *Paluman totut*, it's found across the islands. However, its population is falling.

Coral reefs provide homes for 25 percent of all marine species. The coral reefs around the Northern Marianas are full of amazing creatures, including the largest parrotfish species, the bumphead parrotfish. One area in the archipelago boasts the most number of sharks in a volume of water in the Pacific.

The waters around the island of Saipan have the most variety of coral reefs in the CNMI. Because of the importance of the reefs, the CNMI and the U.S. government recognize the need to protect them from human-caused problems such as pollution and overfishing. In 2009, President George W. Bush established the Marianas Trench Marine National Monument as a refuge, or protected area, in the Marianas archipelago. It protects 95,216 square miles (246,608 sq km) of ocean around the islands.

BUMPHEAD PARROTFISH

MAUG'S CRYSTAL BALL

Maug Island in the CNMI can help scientists see into the future. It's a volcanic caldera that has been flooded by the surrounding ocean. The underwater volcano releases a great deal of the gas called carbon dioxide. By studying Maug, scientists can better understand what will happen to coral reefs as the increase of carbon dioxide in Earth's atmosphere continues. So far, scientists have found that coral, which are living organisms, grow more slowly near areas of higher carbon dioxide.

In addition to being biologically **diverse**, coral reefs protect the coasts of the Northern Mariana Islands from erosion.

Settlers, Explorers, Colonizers

About 3,600 years ago, the ancestors of the people who are called the Chamorros arrived in the Northern Mariana Islands. They came from Southeast Asia. They became farmers and fishers, and sometimes traded with peoples on other islands by boat.

In 1521, Spanish explorer Ferdinand Magellan arrived. It's not certain where exactly, but some believe he landed on Rota, the southernmost of the Northern Mariana Islands. Magellan didn't stay long, but he gave the Mariana Islands the name "Islas de los Ladrones," which is Spanish for "Islands of Thieves," because the Chamorros took one of his boats.

In 1588, British adventurer Thomas Cavendish visited and traded with the islanders. Then, in the 1600s, the Spanish returned to the islands. They took control from the Chamorros, spread their religion and **culture**, and made the Marianas a Spanish colony.

BECOMING A COLONY

A Spanish priest named Diego Luis de Sanvitores arrived in the Northern Marianas in 1668. He renamed the islands "the Marianas" after Mariana of Austria, the queen of Spain who gave him money for his journey. Sanvitores and his followers built churches and schools. Some Chamorros resisted accepting the Catholic religion because they had their own beliefs. Fighting began. Many, including Sanvitores, died in the Spanish-Chamorro Wars, which lasted 26 years. This resistance brought more Spanish—and colonization—to the islands.

Chamorro villages were made up of one-floor houses set on top of rows of two-stone columns. The Chamorro *lattes*, or pillars, have two parts, a base and a top that looks like a cup.

From Spain to Germany to Japan

The Spanish tried to erase Chamorro culture. By the end of the 1600s, they had forced the Chamorros to move to Guam and rebuild their lives according to Spanish culture. By 1820, the Chamorro, who had once numbered between 50,000 and 100,000, had a population of about 1,000. They weren't allowed to return to the Northern Marianas until the mid-1800s.

In 1898, Spain and the United States went to war. Spain lost Guam in the war and sold the Northern Mariana Islands to Germany in 1899. Germany wanted oil from coconuts grown on the islands. The islands were also an important stop on trade routes.

But during World War I (1914–1918), Japan took over the Marianas. The Japanese tightly controlled the islands, overseeing **sugarcane** farms and **refineries**. As many as 40,000 Japanese people moved there.

AGHURUBW, THE CAROLINIAN CHIEF

Aghurubw was a 19th-century chief who lived on the Caroline Islands, south of the Marianas archipelago. When the island of Satawal in the Carolines was destroyed by a typhoon, Aghurubw led his people to what's today the Northern Mariana Islands in small boats. With Spanish permission, they settled on Saipan around 1815. Descendants of these Carolinians still live in the CNMI. Chief Aghurubw was buried on Mañagaha Island, where a monument of him was raised and can be visited today.

The Japanese forced the Germans on the Northern Mariana Islands to leave. This stamp from 1901 is a reminder of Germany's occupation of the islands. The German word Marianen means "Marianas."

World War II Battleground

World War II began in 1939. After Japan bombed Pearl Harbor in Hawaii in 1941, the United States entered the war.

The United States led an invasion of Japanese territories in the Pacific. The two sides waged war on Saipan from June 15 to July 9, 1944. U.S. and Japanese forces battled on land and in the sky in war planes. About 29,000 Japanese soldiers died, and thousands of civilians as well. Rather than be captured, some chose to jump from the high Banzai Cliff on the northern end of the island into the Pacific Ocean. About 3,000 American soldiers were killed and more than 10,000 were injured. After the Americans captured the island, it became a key military air base.

Territorial Truths ☆☆☆☆☆

The United States needed airstrips, or runways, on Pacific islands from which to launch an attack on Japan. Planes needed a place to refuel after long flights over the ocean.

U.S. military vehicles head for shore on June 15, 1944. The USS *Birmingham* is in the foreground, and the cruiser firing in the background is the USS *Indianapolis*.

On July 24, 1944, a few weeks after the U.S. victory on Saipan, American marines landed on the island of Tinian in the Northern Marianas. Fighting between the U.S. and Japanese soldiers there was bitter, and thousands of Japanese soldiers and civilians died. By August 1, the United States declared the island secure. Along with Saipan and Guam to the south, it became an important base for the U.S. Air Force.

On August 6, 1945, a U.S. bomber plane took off from Tinian and headed toward Japan. The B-29 plane, called *Enola Gay*, carried an atomic bomb that it dropped on the city of Hiroshima. Three days later, another bomber, *Bockscar*, departed Tinian. This B-29 dropped an atomic bomb on the Japanese city Nagasaki. Together, more than 100,000 people were killed in the strikes.

Territorial Truths ☆☆☆☆☆

Japan officially surrendered on September 2, 1945, after the bombing of Hiroshima and Nagasaki, ending World War II.

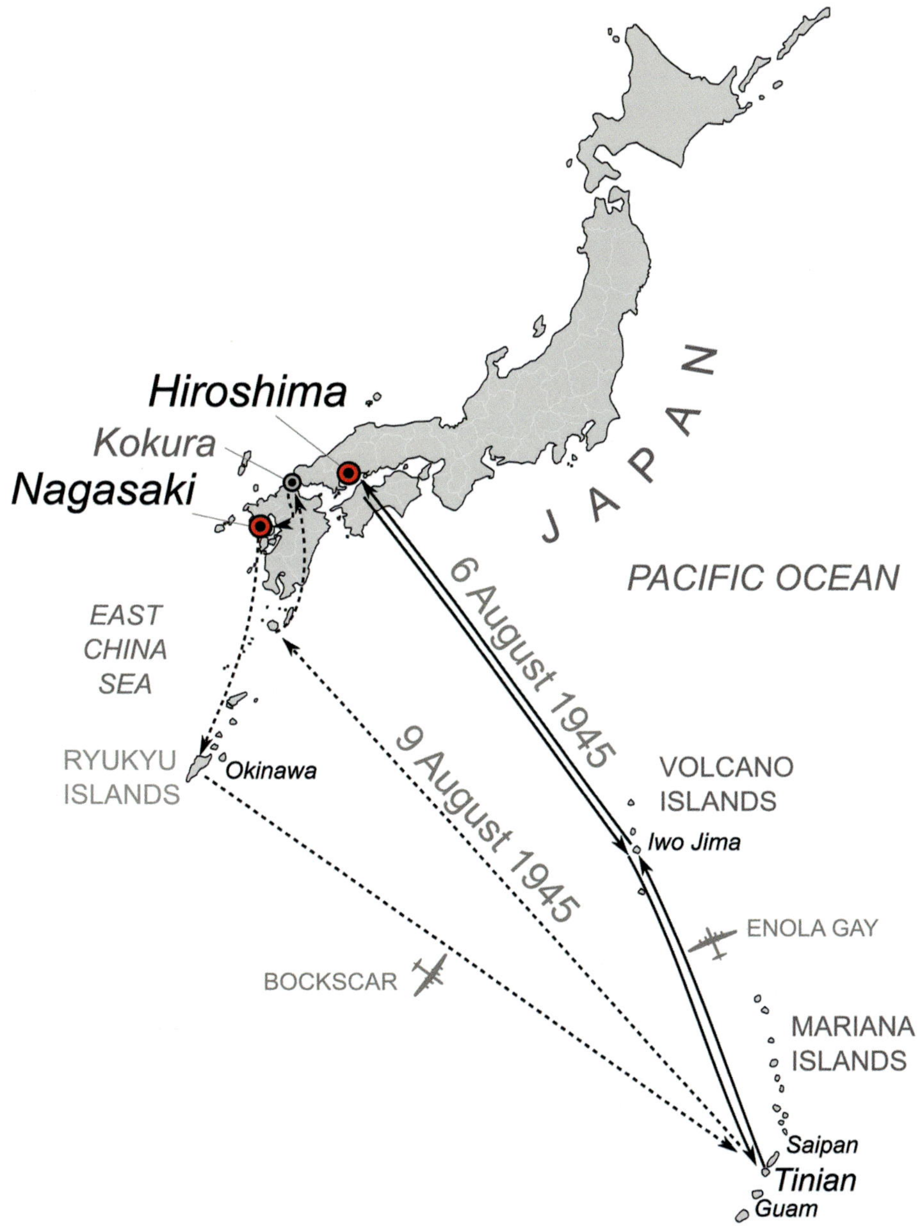

This map shows the atomic-bomb missions that took off from Tinian. The city of Kokura was the original target of the bomb dropped on Nagasaki. However, cloud cover over Kokura changed the mission.

Becoming the CNMI

After World War II, the Northern Mariana Islands became a United Nations territory called a trusteeship. As a trust, it was overseen by U.S. officials while working toward self-government. In 1975, the Northern Marianas voted to become a U.S. commonwealth. This meant it had some self-government, but its citizens were U.S. citizens. The CNMI has its own **constitution**, governor, and legislature with a senate and house of representatives. Some islands have local governments too.

Beginning in the late 1900s, the Northern Mariana Islands became known for clothing production. People from all over Asia worked there, though working conditions were poor and wages low. When U.S. laws to improve workers' lives took effect, some clothing businesses closed or moved where manufacturing was cheaper. Today, tourism is the largest part of the economy.

LIMITED REPRESENTATION

The CNMI is a U.S. territory, not a state. This means that residents can't vote for U.S. presidents. The islands also don't have U.S. senators. The CNMI has one representative to speak for its citizens in the U.S. House of Representatives. This delegate can vote on legislation, but only as part of committees. Some people are working to change this. They want citizens in U.S. territories to have the same voting rights as those who live in states.

The Commonwealth of the Northern Mariana Islands flag features the *latte* stone from Chamorro history, a star that stands for U.S. protection, and a Carolinian flower wreath called a *mwáár*.

A Diverse Population

The CNMI's history has made its population diverse. Today, Chamorros make up about one-fourth of the residents. Some have Spanish, Mexican, Filipino, or other Asian and European ancestry. Filipinos make up about one-third of the islands' population. Chinese, Koreans, Americans, Carolinians, and other Pacific Islanders make up smaller fractions. More than one-half of the people on the CNMI are workers who aren't considered residents. They're mostly from Asian countries. About 90 percent of the total population of the Northern Mariana Islands live on Saipan.

The official languages of the islands are Chamorro, Carolinian, and English. However, many people speak Filipino, languages of the Philippines, and Chinese. The main religions of the islands are Roman Catholicism, **Protestantism**, and **Buddhism**. Some native peoples practice traditional beliefs as well.

Territorial Truths ☆☆☆☆☆

The **cuisine** of the Northern Mariana Islands reflects its diverse population. Favorites include Filipino noodle dishes, Spanish pastries, Chamorro rice dishes, and Japanese, Korean, and American dishes.

SONGSONG, ROTA

In 2023, an estimated 51,295 people lived on the Northern Mariana Islands.

CNMI Sightseeing

Today, people from all around the world visit the Commonwealth of the Northern Mariana Islands. Many tourists come from China, South Korea, Japan, and the United States. They usually visit the many interesting sites on the main islands of Saipan, Rota, and Tinian.

On Saipan, they can visit Kalabera Cave. This cave's human history goes back more than 3,400 years. It contains ancient Chamorro drawings and human skulls. On Rota, Mount Taipingot is a popular location. It's also called Wedding Cake Mountain because of its many layers. On Tinian, a natural formation called the Blowhole shoots water 30 feet (10 m) into the air. All three islands offer many World War II historical sites, opportunities for swimming and snorkeling in the reefs, and countless beautiful views of the Pacific Ocean.

MOUNT TAIPINGOT

TIMELINE

1600 BCE The Chamorros settle the islands.

1521 CE Spanish explorer Magellan is the first European to visit the Northern Mariana Islands.

1668 Father Sanvitores arrives in the Northern Marianas. Wars between the Chamorro and the Spanish soon begin.

1815 Aghurubw leads Carolinian people to Saipan.

1899 Spain sells the Northern Mariana Islands to Germany.

1914 Japan seizes control of the islands from Germany.

1944 The United States captures Saipan and Tinian during World War II.

1945 U.S. bombers depart Tinian and drop atomic bombs on Hiroshima and Nagasaki.

1947 The United States begins to oversee the Northern Mariana Islands.

1975 Northern Marianas residents vote to become a U.S. commonwealth.

2003 The volcano on Anatahan erupts for the first time in recorded history.

2009 President George W. Bush establishes the Marianas Trench Marine National Monument.

2018 The typhoon Yutu causes terrible destruction on the CNMI.

Glossary

archipelago: An island group.

Buddhism: A religion of eastern and central Asia rooted in the teachings of Gautama Buddha.

commonwealth: A territory that has political or economic connections with another country.

constitution: The basic laws by which a country, state, or territory is governed.

cuisine: A style of cooking.

culture: The beliefs and ways of life of a group of people.

diverse: Differing from each other. Made up of people who are different from each other.

endangered: In danger of dying out.

invasive species: A kind of living thing likely to spread and do harm when placed in a new area.

Protestantism: Having to do with the Christian churches that separated from the Roman Catholic Church in the 1500s.

refinery: A place where unwanted bits of matter are removed from something.

satellite: An object that circles Earth to collect and send information or aid in communication.

sugarcane: A tall grass grown in warm places as a source of sugar.

For More Information

Books

Kaufman, Alexander C. *Earth's Aquarium: Discover 15 Real-Life Water Worlds*. New York, NY: Magic Cat Publishing, 2021.

Morey, Allan. *Exploring the Deep Sea*. Minneapolis, MN: Bellwether Media, Inc., 2023.

Roberts, Russell. *World War II in the Pacific*. Lake Elmo, MN: Focus Readers, 2023.

Websites

Marianas Visitors Authority
www.mymarianas.com
This is a great website to check out CNMI events.

National Geographic Kids: Northern Mariana Islands
kids.nationalgeographic.com/geography/u-s-states-and-territories/article/northern-mariana-islands
Read facts and see more photos of this interesting U.S. territory.

Northern Mariana Islands
www.cia.gov/the-world-factbook/countries/northern-mariana-islands/
The U.S. Central Intelligence Agency offers more information about the economy, government, and people of the islands.

Publisher's note to educators and parents: Our editors have carefully reviewed these websites to ensure that they are suitable for students. Many websites change frequently, however, and we cannot guarantee that a site's future contents will continue to meet our high standards of quality and educational value. Be advised that students should be closely supervised whenever they access the internet.

INDEX